MADE WIT

Other books in this series

Living Places
Good Lives
Rooms with a View
Around the House

MADE WITH OAK

by Jeffrey Weiss
and Herbert H. Wise
with Andrea Alberts

New York · London · Tokyo

International Standard Book Number: 0-8256-3052-5
Library of Congress Catalog Card Number: 75-18143

In Great Britain: Book Sales Ltd., 78 Newman Street, London W1 3LA.

In Canada: Gage Trade Publishing, P.O. Box 5000, 164 Commander Blvd.,
Agincourt, Ontario M1S 3C7.

In Japan: Quick Fox, 4-26-22 Jingumae, Shibuya-ku, Tokyo 150.

In Australia: Quick Fox, 27 Clarendon Street, Artarmon, Sydney,
NSW 2064.

In Germany: Music Sales Gmbh, Kölner Strasse 199, D-5000
Cologne 90, West Germany.

Additional photographs: David Frazier and Suzanne Opton
Book design: Christine Yorke

MADE WITH OAK

Oak furniture, the first widely available and truly American furniture, is enjoying a widespread revival. From its initial manufacture in the 1860's to its mass merchandising in the 1900's, its charm, durability, versatility, and economy have insured its appeal. Collectors, decorators, and people who simply like good value and workmanship have joined the ranks of oak buffs—and continue to do so in ever-increasing numbers.

Oak furniture grew out of the cultural needs of nineteenth-century America. The new technology of the machine shop—the power saw and lathe—coupled with the widespread availability of the wood, combined to meet the needs of the new middle class for distinctive furniture that was attractive, long-lasting, and cheap. Because oak is a tough wood it could be worked to take the most intricate and delicate designs that power machinery could impose on it. The handwork and care that had been crucial to good furniture in an earlier era could be approximated by the new technology. Moreover, any town of even modest size could support a furniture factory, draw on nearby streams or rivers for power, and turn lumber into kiln-dried boards in a matter of weeks. Since most of the trained and sophisticated designers remained in the most populous eastern cities, much of what was produced in these small factories, while similar in overall design and conception, shows great individuality and sometimes even eccentricity.

Itinerant designers would pass from city to city, leaving a pattern to be embossed on a chair, or scrollwork for some massive dining-room sideboard, or a design for a lion's head or a claw foot for a table, or a design for the table itself. Sometimes copied from the "finer" furniture of the time, such designs bear a curiously personal quality that accounts for much of their charm. The ease of adding ornaments (embossments, stampings, or carvings) to the basic piece, and the application of direct steam to the freshly kiln-dried wood allowed the furniture maker to execute the heavy trim and graceful curves that distinguish the backs and legs of otherwise humdrum kitchen chairs or rockers. Technique sometimes outran design, and the desire to use the lathe or the saw to ornament to excess occasionally obscured rather than enhanced the natural quality of the oak. But more often than not, each bureau, bed or kitchen cupboard, each fantastically carved, garlanded, monstrously hooked hall rack or hat stand drew a toughness of character from the wood and the woodworking. The solid, golden, grainy hardness of the wood itself served to compliment and subdue the intricacies of decoration.

Herbert Edlin's well known *What Wood Is That?* contains the following notes about oak: "Oak timber has strongly marked features that make it simple to identify. It is ringporous, and the circles of large pores make the softer, less dense springwood of each annual ring stand out clearly from the harder and denser summerwood. The pores show as deep striations or vessel lines on longitudinal surfaces. The rays are well developed. On the end grain they can be seen as clear straight lines, and they are also visible on a slash-sawn or tangential surface. Sawing or slicing an oak log radially, from the center to the circumference, reveals the rays as broad plates, up to one or two inches deep and almost equally wide. They appear definitely harder and smoother than the rest of the wood and reflect the light so strongly that radial-cut oak can fairly be regarded as two-colored. These rays make the famous 'silver grain' of oak, rightly valued as an ornamental feature. Much oak is quarter-sawn to display it."

The remarkable durability and strength of oak as well as its plentiful use in furniture building, make its present popularity understandable. Oak furniture is widely and even inexpensively available. Pieces bought new sixty or even eighty years ago often have remained in the family—if only as utility furniture in a basement or attic. It is still possible to come across the loveliest oak pieces at "country auctions" for a fraction of what they would bring in the hundreds of oak-furniture stores that are springing up throughout the country. But be warned: New England farmers and townspeople alike view the city slicker as fair game, so be sure you like a piece before you start to bid.

The best buys are often of oak furniture that has been painted or "antiqued"; however, it seems so formidable a task to uncover the wood that these bargains are often neglected. Dealers often bring pocket knives to an auction to scrape a bit of paint off such furniture—do the same, but be discreet. Less chancy methods of determining what lies beneath a coat of paint include inspecting drawer tops and the undersides or insides of bureaus and tables, areas often neglected by amateur painters. Don't be deterred by heavily painted objects: Oak, despite its graininess, is a relatively easy wood to refinish. Its hardness allows you to use a scraper to lift the paint off the surface of the wood, which, if done carefully, minimizes the need for smoothing. Apart from a good commercial paint remover (such as Zip-Strip), rubber gloves and steel wool, the chief ingredient is elbow grease. The best way to remove layers of paint is to brush on as heavy a coat of paint remover as is possible without heavy dripping, allow it to remain until the paint has started to blister, then remove it with a scraper if the surface is flat, steel wool if it is not, before it dries. (Be sure to avoid removers that call for a water rinse. They'll raise the grain of the wood and make the job infinitely harder.) Use the finest grade of steel wool available at your hardware store. Don't use the kind meant for the kitchen, it's too coarse. Continue the process until all the paint is removed—you may have to do this three or four times. An old dissecting kit, dental pick or scalpel are useful for removing paint from inside ridges that are carved or embossed.

You'll often find patchy areas where the wood seems shinier than others: that's where the old varnish or lacquer remains, and all traces of those substances must be removed as well. Then, when all the paint is gone, rub the whole piece with fine steel wool lightly dipped in remover. On pieces that are unpainted but that have turned unpleasantly dark because of too many coats of varnish or lacquer, an application of a solution of half lacquer-thinner and half wood-alcohol will dissolve the old residue. Finally, buy some boiled linseed oil and apply it in light coats over a period of several days and then again whenever the luster of the piece dims. Sandpaper should never be used: It raises the grain and virtually triples the amount of work that has to be done. Similarly, avoid commercial refinishing concerns that dip furniture in chemical vats: This process often bleaches the natural color from the wood, loosens or destroys the joints, raises the grain, and causes the wood to swell, twist, or split. Refinishing oak by hand is sometimes tedious but the results cannot be duplicated by other methods, and the satisfaction of seeing the natural beauty of the wood emerge from under layers of paint repays the effort.

Antique stores are the places where most buyers will make their purchases. Since we are not dealing with authenticated antiques, be wary of any dealer who makes a claim of more than "it's old." Be careful not to buy from a dealer who has his furniture dipped: Check the undersides of pieces for "fluffiness," and look for swollen or split joints. Be cautious about buying for investment: While oak furniture has increased in value—probably by five-fold in as many years—it is not rare enough to be considered intrinsically valuable. You're paying for the piece itself—its beauty, distinctiveness and condition. The price guide that follows the photographs is meant to be only the roughest approximation of what you should pay. It shows a range of prices for unpainted, solid wood pieces in good condition at the stores of antique dealers in New England and in New York City. You should expect to pay substantially less at an auction or for a piece that has been painted. But be prepared for wide variance in price from dealer to dealer and from auction to auction. For purposes of illustration and information, line drawings and original prices and descriptions come from the 1902 Sears, Roebuck and Co. catalog. The modern prices are readily apparent.

The photographs on the following pages show the marvelous versatility of oak furniture. From rustic communes to the most elegant lofts and town houses, oak can be used to bring warmth and beauty to virtually any room. The people whose homes are shown here were all unfailingly gracious and kind to us, and we wish to acknowledge our appreciation and gratitude for their help.

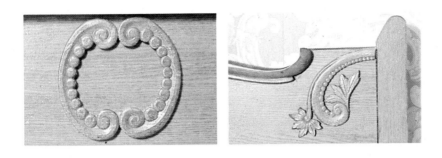

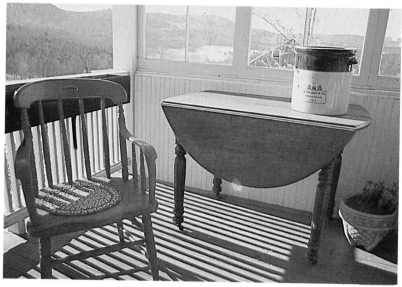

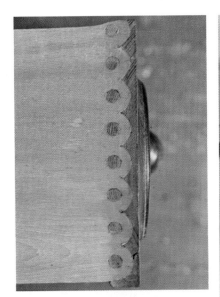

OUR DINING ROOM AND KITCHEN CHAIRS

are strictly high grade, made for us under contract by the best maker in America. Order these chairs from us and you will find for quality of wood, strength, style and finish, you cannot equal them elsewhere at within 50 per cent of our price.

SPECIAL LEADERS IN DINING ROOM AND KITCHEN CHAIRS.
Our 45-Cent Chair.

No. 1R3 The Wood Seat Chair shown in the illustration is especially well constructed and neatly striped. This is a kitchen chair that can seldom be obtained at retail at 65 cents. Our special price is made with a view of proving our ability to render better value than any other house in existence. This chair is made with four spindles, bow back, fancy ornamental stripes. It is made of hardwood and finished in golden oak.
Our special price, each....... ....45c

$15-$40

63 Cents Buys this Handsome $1.00 Dining Chair.

No. 1R9 At the above price we are offering a diner which for solid construction, handsome design and style will compare favorably with chairs offered by many dealers at even double our price. Made of select stock, carefully seasoned. It is durable, put up by one of the best manufacturers, and is very choice. The workmanship is that which only skilled wood workers can produce. This chair is well finished and the handsome carving adds greatly to its appearance. Fancy spindles in back, solid wood seat and strong, well braced legs. Golden oak finish. Our special price, each.....63c

$15-$40

OUR 95-CENT LEADER.

THIS HANDSOME NEW 1902 DESIGN is one of our most serviceable and comfortable dining room chairs. It is solid, yet rich and handsome in appearance; has a large, comfortable back, flat steam bent slats, upper back panel richly carved, has a full shaped seat; in fact, it is offered as the greatest chair value ever offered by us or any other house.
No. 1R11 Our price, each..... 95c

$15-$40

Our $1.10 Leader.

No. 1R12 For $1.10 we offer this unusually rich and attractive Dining Room Chair, with beautifully carved back, exactly as illustrated, as the equal of chairs that will sell in regular furniture stores at $2.00 and $2.25. $1.10 is a price figured on the actual cost of material and labor with but our one small percentage of profit added. This chair is made especially broad and roomy. Has full braced arms, full shaped seat; it is strong and durable as a chair can be made, and with ordinary usage will last a lifetime.
No. 1R12 Our special price, each...........$1.10

$15-$40

New Pattern High Back Wood Seat Chair.

No. 1R13 This is a new pattern of High Back Wood Seat Chair. The design is one of the handsomest of the many we are showing this season. Made of best quality of rock elm, thoroughly seasoned; high back posts and spindles are of graceful design; the top is large and handsomely carved; it has a comfortable seat and is secure; the legs are well braced by nine stretchers of pleasing design. The finish is gloss and is better than most of the so called polish finishes. Price, each......$1.15

$15-$40

Our 99-Cent Cane Seat Wonder.

No. 1R15 This our 99-Cent New Design Cane Seat Dining Room Chair, we offer in competition with and equal to chairs that will be offered everywhere by furniture dealers at prices varying from $1.50 to $2.50. This handsome dining room chair is made from solid oak and beautifully finished golden. It has a hand woven cane seat and brace arm. The back is beautifully turned and carved, as illustrated, producing an ornamental finish. It is made by one of the finest furniture manufacturers in the country whose name is a guarantee for material. Our special price.. ......99c

$15-$40

Our $1.25 Diner.

No. 1R19 This is an unusually attractive cane seat chair; with the latest style hand carved heavy back panel, supported by full braced and fancy turned posts and spindles. Full cane seat, making it a special bargain at the price we quote. One of the newest and best patterns, and made in best selected rock elm. Finished golden.
Price, each ..$1.25

$15-$40

No. 1R27 An Unusually Rich and Attractive Dining Room Chair, beautiful quarter sawed oak in back panels, and broad and roomy full braced arms, and full, fine woven cane seat. As strong and durable as a chair can be made and will last a lifetime. Cannot be duplicated for $2.00. Our price, each.........................$1.47

$15-$40

At $1.60 an Extraordinary Chair Value.

No. 1R33 The handsomest chair ever shown for the money. You have never seen its equal. This is no mistake. We guarantee to furnish you a chair exactly like the one we represent. It is fine enough to adorn the best of homes. Cannot fail to suit the most fastidious. Note the excellent features: Rich hand carvings on back panels, full braced arms, fancy turned spindles. apron front; made of selected rock elm with handsome golden oak finish with full fine woven cane seat. A chair that cannot fail to impress everyone, owing to its beauty and many excellent features.
No. 1R33 Price, each.........................$1.60

$15-$40

Cane or Leather Seat Dining Room Chairs.

A chair that is finely made, comfortable, fashionable and durable, made of very finest quality of golden oak, quarter sawed. Has a fine piano polish, richly carved back, and the best hand made cane seat, full boxed. French legs, plain, substantial and elegant.
No. 1R37 Price, each.... $2.35
No. 1R38 Leather Seat.
Price, each................. 2.95

$15-$40

Our $1.50 University Chair.

No. 1R200 This Chair is thoroughly well made from very fine selected oak. The back and arms are extra well braced by means of iron rods passing through the seat. The chair is decidedly comfortable, and after being once used is considered an absolute necessity. Wood seat, perfectly finished.
Our special price $1.50

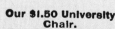

$15-$40

Office Chairs, Screw and Spring Base.

No. 1R208 Office Chair. Is very comfortable, thoroughly well made and handsome in appearance. The back posts are well bolted to seat. Cane seat is hand woven, and the spring may be adjusted to any degree of tension desired, while the chair may be raised or lowered by means of the screw in steel plate. This chair is made of the very finest rock elm and finished golden oak.
Our special price, each......$3.25

$65-$85

Our $4.45 Office Chair.

No. 1R212 A Large, Comfortable, High Back Office Chair. Carved top and front; made of best selected quarter sawed oak, finished golden; has the best patented screw and spring base, and is strong, durable and comfortable.
Price, each.............$4.45

$80-$135

$5.20 Buys a $6.75 Office Chair.

This chair would retail at $6.75 to $8.25. We save you $1.50 to $3.00.
No. 1R214 A Large, Comfortable and Roomy High Back Office Chair. Carved top and front, bent slats in back, made of best selected rock elm, finished golden; has the best patented screw and spring base, and is strong and durable. Price. $5.20

$80-$135

Our Desk Stools.

No. 1R223 The Desk Stool which we illustrate is substantially made, strongly braced, handsome golden oak finished, and has an excellent appearance. It is made of very fine rock elm, kiln dried. It is an excellent stool for the money and cannot be secured for less than 50 per cent above our price.
No. 1R226 24 inches high, wood seat. Price. .65
No. 1R227 24 inches high, cane seat. Price. .90
No. 1R228 33 inches high, wood seat. Price. .90
No. 1R229 33 inches high, cane seat. Price. 1.10

$20-$40

90-Cent Nursery Chair.

No. 1R250 This Chair is really a household necessity, and no family with children should be without one. It is made up of the best rock elm, handsomely decorated, has full back with three spindles. It is strongly constructed, and finished either in regular or antique oak or red.
Our special price, each.................90c

$40-$60

Our $1.15 Child's Rocker.

No. 1R262 Child's Rocker. The comfortable back is beautifully carved and has an elegant appearance. The arms are securely attached to back and seat. Seat is wood, legs are strong and well braced the rockers are securely attached to them We make this rocker of the very best kiln dried elm and finish it in antique oak.
Our special price, each.............$1.15

$40-$60

Our $1.10 High Chair.

No. 1R275 You will see from the illustration that it is strongly built and very handy. This chair is made of the best rock elm, kiln dried and thoroughly seasoned, adjustable table, which swings over child's head so that the child can be placed in the chair before adjusting the table. The chair is finished either in red or antique, as may be desired.
Our special price, each.......$1.10

$40-$60

Latest Style Child's High Chair.

Our Latest Style Child's High Chair, here illustrated, is made with either wood or cane seat. It has large drop table and is made of thoroughly seasoned golden oak, highly finished, making it one of the best grades on the market. The back panel and posts are deeply and elegantly carved.

No. 1R277 Wood Seat. Our special price.................................$1.69
No. 1R278 Cane Seat. Our special price.................................$1.90

$55-$95

Combination High Chair and Carriage, $2.45.

A Combination High Chair and Carriage that is perfect and never gets out of order. Easily changed from a stationary high chair, which will not roll, to a low go-cart, making a very useful piece of furniture. This chair has wide carved back panel and has dark golden oak finish. We have greatly reduced the price, which will cause this chair to be a great favorite the coming season.

No. 1R279 Our reduced price.$2.45

$55-$95

Wonderful Value at $1.75.

PRICE THIS GRADE AT ANY RETAIL FURNITURE STORE

No. 1R202 A Roomy and Comfortable High Back Chair, a steam bent braced arm and nicely carved back panel; has wood seat, and is strongly made and well finished, of the best rock elm, finished golden.
Price, each, $1.75

$50-$75

Best In the World for $3.90.

This is one of those handsome pieces that make the home beautiful. It is large and comfortable, elegantly carved back and panel front and of unusually attractive design. Frame is made of selected quartered golden oak or birch with mahogany finish; has full upholstered seat and back, covered in three-toned velours.

No. 1R349 Price, each, oak.................................$3.90
No. 1R350 Price, each, mahogany finish.............$3.95

$75-$150

Antique or Mahogany Finish Large Rocker for $1.50.

No one will believe it possible to produce such a Rocker for $1.50. One of the most extraordinary bargains ever offered at the price. We save you at least 50 per cent of what many a local dealer would charge you. Made of finest selected rock elm, carefully seasoned, and constructed by the most expert cabinet makers. This rocker will prove an ornament anywhere. The heavily carved panel back is handsome in design, while the neat turned spindles add greatly to the appearance of the chair. The bent arms are braced with iron rods. While the rocker is graceful in outline, it is very strongly made and will last a lifetime. We finish it in either antique or mahogany, as desired. In ordering be sure to state which finish you want.

No. 1R306 Our price, antique finish........$1.50
No. 1R307 Our price, mahogany finish........1.55

Ladies' Sewing Rockers.

Exceptional value. A beautifully carved Rocker, with fancy shaped top, fancy turned posts and spindles. Made of rock elm, finished golden oak. A very well made, serviceable chair. Retails regularly at $2.50.

No. 1R308 With wood seat. Our special price.............$1.40
No. 1R310 Same chair as No. 1R308, excepting it has cane seat. Our special price...........$1.55

$75-$150

Beautifully Carved Cobbler Seat Rocker, In Antique or Mahogany Finish.

In this handsome and especially well made Cobbler Seat Rocker, we are offering a rare bargain. This rocker is made of selected rock elm, with high carved back of handsome design, fancy turned spindles, easy and comfortable cobbler seat of embossed leather. Extra large, with bent arms. Securely braced with iron rods. A most ornamental and durable addition to parlor or library. Made either in antique or mahogany finish. In ordering be sure to say which finish you want.

No. 1R313 Our price, antique finish........$1.75
No. 1R314 Our price, mahogany finish......1.80

$75-$150

One of Our Big Bargains for $3.15.

The manufacturer put it into our power to sell this high grade rocker, such as you can get at no other place at anything like the price. Made of the finest quality of golden oak or mahogany. Highly hand polished, has elaborately hand carved back and fancy turned spindles, the latest fancy colored embossed leather seat, well braced and fancy turned arms, and with ordinary care is guaranteed to last a lifetime.

No. 1R339 Price, each, golden oak.................................$3.15
No. 1R340 Price, each, mahogany finish....$3.20

$75-$150

The Farmer's Friend.

You can scarcely believe it is possible to secure such a large, roomy rocker as shown in this illustration, for the extremely low price quoted. It is hand carved and polished and has heavy steam bent arm posts and slat spindles; it is well braced in every way and has dark golden oak finish. The large seat and high shaped back makes this chair very comfortable and desirable.

No. 1R321 Our special price, wood seat.................$2.95
No. 1R322 Our special price, cane seat.....................3.40
No. 1R323 Our special price, genuine leather seat.................................$4.35

$75-$150

Our $3.45 Golden Oak Rocker.

No. 1R346 A beautiful rocker of the latest pattern. Large and comfortable, with high paneled back richly carved. Made of the best seasoned and selected quarter sawed golden oak, elegantly finished, making a rocker that will be an ornament to any room.

Our special price......$3.45

$75-$150

Elegant Rocker for $2.25.

A Rocker that in appearance is one of the most striking and handsome we are showing this season. Has high back, richly carved panels, steam bent braced arms, and full shaped seat. Is unusually well made; rock elm, and finished in golden elm or imitation mahogany.

No. 1R318 Price, each, golden elm................$2.25
No. 1R319 Our price, mahogany finished.................$2.30

$75-$150

Our Special $2.50 Rocker.

No. 1R320 A beautiful high back fully carved Rocker, with full cobbler leather seat. Made of the best selected oak, finished golden; broad and roomy and very comfortable. Also made in mahogany finish.

Price.........................$2.50

$75-$150

Our $4.60 Veneered Rocker.

Another of those beautiful veneer Rockers of superb design; finished golden oak, quarter sawed or imitation mahogany. The panels are richly carved and spindles are of fancy turnings. It is very pretty, and will adorn any parlor.

No. 1R414 Price, each, oak.................................$4.60
No. 1R415 Price, each, mahogany finish.............$4.65

$75-$150

$5.40 Buys This Handsome Veneered Rocker.

Imitation mahogany and quartered golden oak, veneered seat and back, polished. One of our most handsome and attractive up to date rockers, very roomy and comfortable, neatly carved, has pretty curved seat, neat carvings on panel, is very strong and durable.

No. 1R420 Price, quarter sawed golden oak..$5.40
No. 1R421 Price, imitation mahogany......5.45

$75-$150

Veneered Fancy Rockers.

Made in quarter sawed golden oak or veneered imitation mahogany, as desired. An artistic, fancy rocker, new, novel and very comfortable; full shaped seat, strongly braced, elegant in appearance and will give service and comfort.

No. 1R412 Price, in quarter sawed golden oak, each...$2.93
No. 1R413 Price, in imitation mahogany, each.....$2.98

$75-$150

Invalids' Chair.

No. 1R206 This Highly Finished Invalids' Chair has high back and arms with box under the seat which opens from the back, and is large enough for any chamber. This is a very convenient piece of furniture for any sick room, and no family should be without one. Our special price...$3.40

$50-$75

Our $8.20 and $8.95 Solid Oak Bookcase.

From the small illustration by our artist from a photograph, you can get some idea of this handsome case. It is made of carefully selected, quarter sawed golden oak finish or imitation mahogany as desired. This handsomely carved and trimmed case has high piano finish, is made with durable shelves and nice back; handsome top ornamentation; extra heavy glass in doors. Is 65 inches high and 37 inches wide. At our special $8.20 price we furnish it complete with handsome pattern, bevel French plate mirror, 6x16 inches. In ordering be sure to state whether you wish quarter sawed oak or imitation mahogany. Shipping weight, 115 pounds.

No. 1R1302 Price, without mirror $8.20
No. 1R1304 Price, with mirror complete... 8.95

Our $6.95 Oak Bookcase.

Retails everywhere at $10.00.

No. 1R1301 Bookcase, 57 inches high and 32 inches wide, is made of quartered golden oak, with handsome golden oak finish. The door is of double thick glass, the shelves are adjustable, the back is of solid oak and well finished inside. This is the cheapest bookcase made for the money. Shipping weight, 90 pounds.

Price $6.95

Our $7.45 Library Table.

No. 1R1252 Library Table, made of golden oak, or birch finished in a beautiful shade of mahogany; has heavy twisted legs with large shelf and one drawer, fitted with best cast brass handle. Size of top, 26x46 inches; a high grade table at a very low figure; stock is select and handsome; a good sensible style. Weight, about 65 pounds. Price, $7.45

Our $5.00 Desk.

No. 1R1404 A Neat and Attractive Writing Desk of the finest quarter sawed oak. Neat, pretty carvings. Interior arranged for papers, stationery, etc. Is 27 inches wide. Weight, 50 pounds.

Price.............$5.00

No. 1R556 This Round Top Pillar Extension Table is one of the latest designs for 1902, and will compare favorably with Pillar tables which are offered by other dealers at double the price we quote. This table is made of solid oak. The top measures 42 inches in diameter, and is rubbed finish. Shipping weight, 165 pounds

Price, 6-foot table $10.35
Price, 8-foot table......................... 11.25
Price, 10-foot table........................ 12.15
Price, 12-foot table........................ 13.10

No. 1R560 The illustration shows our prettiest design, a Pillar Round Top Extension Table. It is made of solid oak, beautifully finished. The top of the table measures 46 inches in diameter, and is beautifully ornamented with beaded molding, while the legs are handsomely carved and ornamented, making it one of the most attractive tables which we can furnish. Shipping weight, about 175 pounds.

Price, 6-foot table.......................$12.45
Price, 8-foot table........................ 13.35
Price, 10-foot table....................... 14.25
Price, 12-foot table....................... 15.20

No. 1R552 This Table is made of solid oak. Top measures 42 inches in diameter. The legs measure 6 inches in diameter and are handsomely turned and fluted, as shown in the illustration. This table is one of the most substantial extension tables it is possible to procure, and will be sure to please the most exacting customer. Shipping weight, about 195 pounds.

Price, 6-foot table .... $ 9.95
Price, 8-foot table......................... 10.90
Price, 10-foot table........................ 11.85
Price, 12-foot table........................ 12.80

No. 1R568 For massiveness and solidity there is nothing to equal this most beautifully and elaborately designed table. This is one of the handsomest of our line; has five large, massive legs with the richest and most elaborate tracing and carving and is very strong. Made of the best quality solid golden oak. The top is 46x46 inches when closed. Fitted with improved ball bearing casters. Weight, packed for shipment, 210 pounds.

Price, 8-foot table........................... $13.95
Price, 10-foot table.......................... 14.90
Price, 12-foot table.......................... 15.85

No. 1R572 This Table is made from carefully selected extra heavy quarter sawed golden oak, rubbed and polished to a piano finish. Has five massive hand turned and beaded legs; fancy trimmings on all four sides; has a very large heavy top, 45x45 inches in size. Legs are fitted with improved ball bearing casters. This is one of the handsomest tables shown this season, regardless of price. It is a table you must see, examine and compare with others to appreciate its real worth. Shipping weight, 225 pounds.

Price, 8-foot table........................$13.95
Price, 10-foot table....................... 15.50
Price, 12-foot table....................... 17.10

No. 1R532 This Extension Table is made of solid oak; golden finish. The top measures 42x42 inches when closed. As shown in the illustration it has six massive, fancy turned legs, the end ones being joined by a handsomely carved stretcher, which adds greatly both to the appearance and strength of the table. Complete with casters. Shipping weight, about 165 pounds.

Price, 6-foot table $5.25
Price, 8-foot table......................... 6.15
Price, 10-foot table....................... 7.05
Price, 12-foot table........................ 8.95

Our $14.60 Extension Table.

No. 1R576 Order this table and if you do not find it one of the richest, handsomest and altogether best tables in your section, and about one-half the price charged by others, you can return it at our expense and we will return your money. This is such a table as you will find only in the finest city retail stores. It is made of elegantly finished quarter sawed oak, highly polished. Top is 45x45 inches. Has very heavy, massively finished 7¼-inch legs fitted with the very latest improved ball bearing casters. This table comes either square as illustrated, or with round top as desired. In ordering, be sure to state whether you wish square or round top. Shipping weight, 225 pounds.

Price, 8-foot table....	$14.60
Price, 10-foot table.....	15.70
Price, 12-foot table........	17.80

No. 1R578 Same table as above, with 48x48-inch top, round or square, as desired, extra $2.00.

No. 1R520 The Old Fashioned Round Drop Leaf Table, which we show in the illustration, is an old time favorite and never goes out of date; nor does it lose any of its desirable features. It is made of solid oak, with an oval top, the size of which is 42x52 inches. Can be taken apart and shipped knocked down, thus saving very largely in the freight rate. It comes in three sizes at the following prices. Complete with casters. Weight, about 100 pounds.

Price, 6-foot table............	$4.45
Price, 8-foot table............	5.35
Price, 10-foot table........	6.25

No. 1R544 This Table is made of solid oak. It has five handsomely turned 5-inch legs. Top measures 42x42 inches when closed. This table is finished in antique. Complete with casters. Shipping weight, about 175 pounds.

Price, 6-foot table...........	$ 7.80
Price, 8-foot table...........	8.75
Price, 10-foot table...........	9.70
Price, 12-foot table...........	10.65

Combination Case and Writing Desk, $12.70.

No. 1R1321 This Handsome Combination Bookcase is made of the finest quarter sawed golden oak and is very attractive in design; is richly carved; has shaped bevel mirror, 12x14 inches; has three roomy drawers and has four adjustable shelves; large writing lid; interior of desk nicely arranged for stationery; full double glass front; is 74 inches high and 41 inches wide; complete with locks, best trimmings, and casters, etc. Weight, 165 pounds. Price, each, $12.70.

$6.20 Buys this Handsome Desk that Furniture Stores Ask $10.00 For.

No. 1R1434 This Handsome Desk is made of fine, carefully selected and thoroughly seasoned oak; has high golden antique finish; has three drawers with drop table to write on, and drawers and table are fitted with locks and brass pulls. The cabinet is conveniently divided; it has a compartment for books, papers and writing material and one pull drawer in center. The best construction throughout. The height of the desk is 4 feet 8 inches; width, 2 feet 6 inches. It is beautifully polished and finished with scroll carvings, an extremely useful and ornamental piece of furniture. Shipped from our factory in Central Illinois. Weight, 80 pounds.
Our price.................$6.20

Our $9.45 Ladies' Writing Desk.

Ladies' Desk; 4 feet 10 inches high, 29 inches wide; with 8x14-inch French bevel plate mirror. This desk is made of solid oak, partly quarter sawed. Also made in birch, and is finished in a high gloss finish, either in antique oak or imitation mahogany. The inside is pigeonholed, and has one drawer in center, also two large drawers and upper shelf. The hand carving is beautiful, and the trimmings are of brass. Casters are ball bearing. Shipping weight, 100 pounds.
No. 1R1420 Price, in oak..........$9.45
No. 1R1422 Price, each, in mahogany finish..........$9.75

Our $19.95 High Grade Curtain Desk.

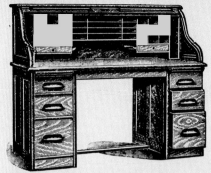

High Curtain Office Desk, 4 feet 6 inches long, 2 feet 6 inches wide, 4 feet 1 inch high; well made, of solid oak and polished. Has lap joint, dust and knife proof curtain, a solid oak writing bed. Oak, finished antique; extension slides, finished back, quarter sawed sycamore pigeonhole case. Combination lock on drawers, spring lock with duplicate keys on curtain; three drawers on each side, deep bottom drawers partitioned for books; two drawers, pen rests and card racks in interior; also with closed panel back to order. Weight, 185 pounds.
No. 1R1467 Price, 4-foot...................$19.95
No. 1R1468 Price, 5-foot...................21.45

A Solid Oak, Flat Top Desk for $8.95.

This Desk is made of solid oak, is 54 inches long, 30 inches wide and 30 inches high. It measures 24 inches between the pedestals and has four drawers on the left side and one drawer on the right side over the cupboard, which is arranged for books and papers. The top of the desk is made up of built up wood, insuring it against warping or splitting. This desk is undoubtedly one of the greatest values in flat top desks ever offered by any dealer. Shipping weight, 150 pounds.
No. 1R1442 Our special price...................$8.95
No. 1R1444 Same Desk as No. 1R1442, excepting that it is only 48 inches long instead of 54 inches. Our special price...................$8.45

Our $9.25 Flat Top Office Desk.

No. 1R1450 This Flat Top Office Desk is made of solid oak, beautifully finished, heavy paneled sides and back, imitation leather top. Size, 4 feet 2 inches by 30 inches. Has four drawers, fitted with lock and key, heavy piano legs, well made and finished throughout. Weight, 150 pounds. Price, each..$9.25

Great Value at $15.50.

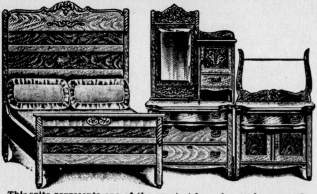

This suite represents one of the greatest bargains we have ever been able to offer in the shape of a three-piece suite with cheval dresser. We embody in this suite the latest ideas of the best designers and manufacturers of bedroom furniture. The dresser and commode have the double swell top drawers, which together with the handsome carved decorations and brass ornaments make the suite especially attractive. We can furnish the suite in golden oak finish or imitation mahogany as desired. Every piece is supplied with ball bearing casters. The bedstead is 6 feet 6 inches in height, and has 4 feet 6-inch slats. The dresser measures 20x44 inches, and has a fine French bevel plate mirror 16x26 inches in size. The size of the top of the washstand is 17x33 inches, and is constructed to correspond with the bed and dresser.

We ship this suite direct from our factory in Northern Indiana, but reserve the privilege of forwarding same from our store when convenient.

No. 1R1634 Weight, 100 pounds. Price of bed............... $3.75
No. 1R1635 Weight, 100 pounds. Price of dresser............ 8.35
No. 1R1636 Weight, 50 pounds. Price of commode............ 3.40
No. 1R1637 Price of complete suite.................... **$15.50**

$180-$375

One of Our Handsomest and Latest Design Bedroom Suites for $16.95.

For only $16.95 we offer this very handsome, beautifully carved, elegantly finished three-piece Bedroom Suite, as one of the very best values in our entire stock. This suite should not be compared with suites offered by other dealers at anywhere near our price, as it is equal in quality and finish to suites that retail regularly at $28.00 to $35.00. It is made of solid oak, handsomely carved and decorated, as shown in the illustration. The trimmings are best quality brass, and each piece is fitted with ball bearing casters. The bed is full size, and measures 6 feet 4 inches in height and 4 feet 6 inches in width. The dresser measures 20x44 inches, and has double deck top, double swell top drawers and two large, roomy straight front drawers. The handsomely shaped mirror is French bevel plate, 22x28 inches. The commode is 18x34 inches, has splasher back and swell drawer to match the dresser, besides two lower drawers and a roomy cupboard. We ship this suite direct from our factory in Northern Indiana, but reserve the privilege of shipping from our store when convenient.

No. 1R1658 Weight, 120 pounds. Price of bed............ $4.15
No. 1R1659 Weight, 125 pounds. Price of dresser....... 9.45
No. 1R1660 Weight, 60 pounds. Price of commode....... 3.35
No. 1R1661 Price of complete suite.................... **$16.95**

$180-$375

No. 1R3826 No. 1R3832 No. 1R3838

No. 1R3826 Pier Mirror. Strikingly rich and elegant. Made of select oak, finished in golden oak or curly birch in mahogany finish. Handsome hand carved top, turned pillars. 90 inches high, 28 inches wide. Fitted with French plate, 18x40 inches.

Price, French plain........................... $10.00
Price, French bevel........................... 10.45

No. 1R3832 Pier Mirror, made of select oak, finished in golden oak, carved top and molding; width, 30 inches; height, 93 inches. Fitted with French plate, 20x60 inches.

Price, French plain........................... $13.60
Price, French bevel.. .... 15.35

No. 1R3838 Pier Mirror, made of select oak, finished in golden oak or curly birch in mahogany finish. Highly polished, raised hand carving and rope pillars. Outside measurements—width, 30 inches; height, 93 inches. Fitted with French plate and 4-inch French bevel circle on top of mirror. Size of plate, 20x60 inches.

Price, French plain........................... $17.75
Price, French bevel.......................... 19.95

$100-$175

$3.70 is the Price in Polished Oak.

No. 1R1238 This is a neat and pretty Parlor Table, of excellent design. Has pretty shaped top, rim and legs, lower shelf with fancy carved brackets. Size of top, 22x30 inches, and made of polished oak, finished antique. Price... **$3.70**

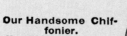

$45-$75

Parlor Stands and Tables.

No. 1R1208 This Handsome Table is made of the best oak, finished antique and piano polished. Size of top, 24x24 inches; has good lower shelf and fancy turned legs; is absolutely first class in construction and finish. Weight, 25 pounds. Price.............. $1.15
No. 1R1209 Same as above, with glass ball and brass feet. Price... .... **$1.50**

$40-$65

Our Handsome Chiffonier.

No. 1R1932 A very ornamental and useful pattern; made of selected antique oak; has three large and two small drawers and one hat box; has a shaped bevel French mirror, 11x17 inches; has a shaped top, 17x32 inches, and is well trimmed and finished. Shipping weight, about 125 pounds. Price, each **$8.15**

$75-$100

Our $7.85 Chiffonier.

No. 1R1929 A Chiffonier that is useful and ornamental; has five large drawers for storage; is made of selected golden oak, well constructed and finished; has 11x17-inch bevel French mirror and serpentine shaped top, 17x30 inches, and neat, pretty trimmings. This is one of the best values in chiffoniers which we offer this season. Shipping weight, about 125 pounds.

Price, each........... **$7.85**

$75-$100

$16.95 for this Handsomely Carved Sideboard.

No. 1R1038 Made of the best golden oak, with a graceful serpentine shaped top, 48 inches long and 24 inches wide; two upper swell front drawers, one lined for silver, and a large linen drawer; is handsomely and boldly carved and has a shaped bevel French plate mirror 16x28 inches; a real bargain. Shipped direct from our factory near Grand Rapids, Mich. Customer pays the freight from the factory. Shipping weight, 175 pounds.

Price, each..... **$16.95**

$125-$175